Ruth's Ducks

Written by Michele Garza
Illustrated by Biva Nguyen
Edited by Lise DeShea

ISBN
979-8-218-07500-2

Ruth's Ducks

Michele Garza

For Ruth, wherever you are
My mom, for saving the ducks
and Harper, *everything* is for you

In Memory of David Vaillancourt

"*Michele, just pick something. Anything,*" my mom mumbled in the toy aisle. She was trying not to sound frustrated.

"*I will, but I want it to be really good,*" I whined, followed with a closed-mouth smile to highlight my dimples, something I knew she found irresistible.

"*Fine, but please hurry.*"

Choosing this around-ten-dollars gender-neutral grab-bag gift was more pressure than my eight-year-old decision-making skills could handle. I combed the aisle examining the prices. I finally decided on a Lisa Frank art set, explaining to her that I would trade what I received if someone picked the art kit and didn't want it. My mom, eager to get home and make dinner, reluctantly agreed.

It was my first semester at a weekly Bible study for kids. We met on Wednesdays in the basement of a local church where they divided us into age groups. Aside from religion, the program also included music and gym class. I started this program halfway through the school year, and though I had not made any friends yet, everyone was warming to me quickly. For the last class before Christmas break, we were instructed to bring a wrapped gift worth ten dollars for a grab-bag exchange. I knew the art set would be a hit because the week before at school, my entire table in the lunchroom said that they had put Lisa Frank on their Christmas lists.

That Wednesday night all anyone wanted to talk about was the gift exchange. I made the conscious effort to talk my gift down. We were unsure of how the exchange would work and I didn't want anyone to know what I had brought, just in case there was a chance I could pick my own gift. *"I don't even know what mine is, my mom picked it and then wrapped it,"* I told the kid next to me. *"It's probably pretty lame."*

After the opening ceremony of songs, my age group had gym. This was the only week when it went by too slowly. I couldn't focus on anything but the anticipation of bringing home a new toy to show off to my siblings. Gym was followed by snacks and Bible study. We would spend the second half of our Bible time on the grab-bag exchange.

When we arrived at our classroom our teacher, Ms. Elizabeth, was waiting for us. I liked her; it was hard not to. Her voice was soft, and her eyes were warm. She had long brown hair with little strands of gray that peeked through. She always wore long skirts that came to just above the top of her sneakers, allowing her socks to show. Her sweatshirts had iron-on Bible character patches that were outlined with puffy paint. She instructed us to put our gifts on the table in the front of the classroom and then sit down. My assigned seat was in the last row. We all stared

intently as Ms. Elizabeth put numbered sticky notes on each gift. She then held up an elf hat and said it was time to begin the grab-bag!

"I'm going to bring this elf hat around the room. It's filled with pieces of paper that have numbers on them. You will each pick one. Then in order from the lowest number to highest, I will call you the table and I will give you the gift that has the same number" Then Ms. Elizabeth told us, *"DO NOT open your gift until everyone has gone and I have told you it is okay."*

13
5
6
23
30

I picked the number three, so I didn't have to wait long for my turn. I approached the table with nervous excitement, my number smudged from the moisture of my hands. I handed my paper to Ms. Elizabeth without saying a word. She picked up a gift, which was not the one that I brought, but equal in size. She pulled the sticky note off it and handed it to me. Overwhelmed with excitement and curiosity, I spun around. Walking back down the aisle I felt all eyes on me. While Ms. Elizabeth called out the next number, everyone in my class sat up straight and stretched their necks out to see what I had gotten. I took my seat with a good feeling. Christmas, the holiday of gift giving, was officially upon us.

When the last gift had been claimed, the teacher said, *"Oh, no! Ruth has gotten her own gift. Will someone please exchange with her?"* I looked over at a girl holding a box that was twice the size of mine. The wrapping paper was gold and it glistened in the fluorescent lights. It had a large green bow, not the stick-on kind but one made from real ribbon wrapped vertically and horizontally and tied neatly in the center. I stared down at my tiny package with dull Santas on the wrapping and cheap curled ribbon taped on the top. I greedily decided I needed to have what Ruth was holding. My hand shot up into the air and with a smile that showed all my teeth I shouted, *"I'll exchange with her!"* I hoped no one would challenge my offer. The class grew quiet. Ms. Elizabeth smiled and nodded. I walked over to Ruth and held out my gift with a smirk of victory.

"Michele, that's nice of you, but that's Rebbecca, not Ruth," Ms. Elizabeth whispered in my direction. I looked over my shoulder and saw another girl standing in the front of the class. She was Ruth! Ruth's clothing was too large for her small frame. Her white clothes were yellowed, the blacks were grayed, and the foul sneakers on her feet must have once belonged to her older brother. She was holding a ball of newspaper. Then I remembered. Ruth was the homeschooled girl who kept to herself. I stood there wishing I could take back my offer. The class filled with giggles as I felt my body get warmer. Ruth practically skipped to me and held out her ball of newspaper. I tried not to cry as I handed over the Santas (who didn't seem that dull after all).

I went to the back of the room and sat in my chair once again. Ms. Elizabeth gave us the okay to open our gifts. I unwrapped the ball of paper and found two tiny wax ducks connected with a short wick. The white ducks had yellow beaks and blue bows tied around their necks. Everyone moved around the room showing off their gifts, I looked over at Ruth. She was hugging what she had opened when someone said, *"Ruth! We got the same thing! Lisa Frank!"* My body went from warm to hot as I held back my tears.

In the parking lot I buried my face inside my coat while waiting for our blue station wagon to arrive. The other kids were showing one another the awesomeness they got to take home. The adults wished the teachers happy holidays and talked about vacation plans. I heard our car enter the parking lot. Ours was the one that had the loud engine and a muffler that dragged on the pavement when it hit a sudden incline. My mom always had a smile on her face when she picked me up. The size of her smile was bigger when she was running late. I got in the front seat and slammed the door. I burst into tears holding out Ruth's ducks.

"There is no way these were ten dollars! Right mom?"

"What is that?"

"My grab-bag. The homeschooled girl brought it."

"Michele, I think that is probably something she had at home already."

"WHAT? That's SO not fair," I said, beating my head against the back of my seat.

On the way home my mom explained that Ruth had a large family, and they may not have been able to purchase a new gift for every child in their family to participate in the grab-bag. She also told me that Ruth may not receive many new things for Christmas, and it was wonderful she got something so special. I still thought it was unfair. When we arrived home, I threw the ducks in the trash and stomped to my room. Shortly after, my mom called me downstairs. She was holding the ducks.

"I'm disappointed in you. We may not have as much as some of the kids you know, but we have plenty. These ducks will be our reminder that some people have less than us and to be thankful for what we do have." She placed the ducks over a branch on our Christmas tree as an ornament and said, *"Michele, you may not get it today, but one day you will understand."*

The next year while our family was unpacking our Christmas decorations, my mom came across Ruth's Ducks and asked if I would like to hang them up.

"Toss them out!" I whined.

My mom shook her head with disappointment. *"Okay, not this year, but one day you will understand."*

Hanging Ruth's Ducks became a holiday tradition that I didn't participate in. Shortly after Thanksgiving, my family would gather around our plastic tree fresh from our attic and open our Christmas decoration boxes. When the ducks came out, my mom would always ask me if I would like to hang them up, and every year I said no. Whenever I saw the ducks, I would move them to the back of the tree even though they always managed to make their way front and center again. I would also refuse to acknowledge them when my mom would tell guests how they came into our lives. I hated those dumb ducks.

Then a few years later, my paternal grandmother, my Abuela, passed away. She wasn't the first person I had lost; when I was four my best friend was an elderly neighbor who didn't make it to my fifth birthday. My family had lost several members (mostly grand- and great-grandparents) while I was in elementary school. I had a particularly hard time with my Abuela's passing because I knew how much my dad had depended on her after my parents' divorce. My dad and Abulela helped support one another emotionally and financially and I worried about what he would do to make ends meet. My dad moved from his house to an apartment. He worked two jobs and always had car issues. His muffler didn't drag, it roared. Despite his losses, he always stayed positive and focused on the things he did have.

That same year my mom worked two jobs to make ends meet. At the time it didn't seem like a big deal. Our neighbor Shirley took us to and from school with her kids. We would see our mom between her jobs when we got home in the afternoon. We never did without. Our mom made sure we had everything we needed and wanted (within reason). Oftentimes this meant she was the one who did without.

That Thanksgiving my siblings and I were called into the living room for a family meeting. Our mom looked upset but she was forcing a smile.

"Money is a little tight this year. We're still going to exchange gifts, but there will not be as much as what you are used to, and everything may not be brand new. You're all getting older and need to remember what Christmas is really all about."

Our mom waited for our reactions. She must have heard us looking through the Toys-R-Us catalog making our Christmas lists. Big lists. I thought about how my mom was always working and yet there wasn't money for gifts. She looked worried. My heart sank. Nothing mattered more to me in that moment than wanting to explain to her what I really loved about the holiday season.

What I really loved about Christmas Day was that my little sister came to our house. We were allowed to eat whatever we wanted. Anything at all. One year the three of us kids had a challenge to see who could eat the most Hershey kisses. We all got stomachaches and spent the rest of the night fighting over the bathroom. Lesson learned. What I really loved was that we were together as a family. We played games and made home movies. Normally, my brother was the camera guy while my sister and I pranced around trying to see who could get more camera time. No one had to go to work or school or a friend's house. What I really loved was that we went sledding in our hilly yard and that every time the phone rang, someone wanted to talk to us kids. What I really loved is when we watched *A Christmas Story*, which was extra special to us because it takes place in our hometown. We even went to Warren G. Harding Elementary where Flick gets his tongue stuck to the flagpole!

What I really loved about Christmas Eve (which we normally spent with my dad) was making hundreds of tamales with his side of the family. It was a long-standing family tradition, and everyone was required to help. I was in charge of soaking the *hojas* (husks). Back then I thought it was great, that I was a key part of the process. Now I realize it just kept me out of everyone's way. What I really loved was that after we had dinner, all of the cousins would put on holiday skits and have dance competitions. We got to stay up late and go to church with grandma. She would help me get ready and I would wear a dab of her perfume. Sure, I smelled like an old lady, but it made me feel special. What I really loved was that I always got a new-to-me dress for this occasion and shoes that clicked when I walked. This drove my brother crazy.

"She's making them make that noise on purpose," he'd whine.

"No, I'm not!" I'd say taking exaggerated steps.

What I really loved was that after church Abuela would convince my dad to take us to a diner as a treat for being so good, even if we weren't. Abuela was awesome. Then I remembered this would be my first Christmas without her.

I watched my mom try not to cry, all because she couldn't buy us new toys. It was right at that moment that I remembered Ruth and her family.

My siblings didn't seem fazed. My brother wanted to go back to his video game and my sister asked if we could still help make Christmas dinner. We were assured that there would still be food, which was sufficient for her. Family meeting adjourned.

Later that evening, I found my mom alone in our living room. She had pulled out the Christmas boxes and fake tree by herself. She was playing my favorite Christmas album. I could tell she had been crying. I sat down next to her not knowing what to say. Sitting between us was our well-loved

copy of *The Night Before Christmas.* On top of the book were Ruth's Ducks lying on their sides. I picked them up and dangled them from my finger.

"Can I hang the ducks this year, Mom?" I asked. My mom's eyes filled with tears as she nodded.

Ruth's Ducks never went back into our Christmas decoration boxes again. They hung in my mom's kitchen the eleven months they were not on her Christmas tree. Every year I had to remind her that one day, when I had my own family, she would have to part with the ducks. After all, Ruth gave them to me

ABOUT THIS BOOK

Ruth's Ducks is a true story that originated in Northwest Indiana. Since then, the story and the tradition of hanging Ruth's Ducks has been shared around the world.

During a remedial English course in college, Michele Garza was given a writing prompt to write about a time a material possession taught her a lesson. At the time, she was studying to be an elementary school teacher.

Garza wrote a one-page response about Ruth's Ducks and the meaning behind the tradition in her family. Her boyfriend Robert read the response and suggested she was a writer. That year he purchased Garza writing classes at a workshop based in New York City.

During the workshop, she was encouraged to take writing classes in college, which she did. Almost immediately, she changed her major to English and focused on creative writing.

In a later class, Garza was given an assignment to take a previous piece of writing and turn it into an essay and that's how Ruth's Ducks turned into a longer version of the story.

Garza would go on to share this story with friends and family for over a decade. During the pandemic, an old friend from a Broadway internship, Janine, reached out and asked Garza for her address. Janine sent Garza a package with a note and a bulb ornament with a bunch of ducks on it. She explained that reading Ruth's Ducks was now a part of her holiday traditions and she wanted her own version of Ruth's Ducks for her tree. Janine purchased an extra ornament for Garza.

That is when Garza knew she needed to replicate the ducks into an ornament.

With the help of her TikTok fol§lowers, Garza launched a Kickstarter crowd-sourced fundraiser and raised enough money to hire an illustrator (Biva Nguyen) so that Garza could self-publish/produce the book and ornament. Copies of Ruth's Ducks were purchased by TikTok followers from around the world.

Garza is grateful for everyone who has helped with the greater story of Ruth's Ducks, including David Vaillancourt who was the first person to suggest turning the original essay into a fully illustrated Children's Book.

Through social media, there was a campaign to find Ruth. At the time of this publication, she had not come forward.

MICHELE GARZA

grew up in Northwest Indiana in a family that was able to shield her from some of their financial hardships. She graduated with a BA in English from Hunter College (CUNY). She currently resides in St. Charles, Illinois, with her daughter Harper and their pets, Wrigley and Stripey. Ruth's Ducks sit on her writing desk the eleven months they are not on her Christmas tree.

The original set of Ruth's Ducks now lives in a protective case.

Photo Credits: Amy Adelsen